# GOD'S LITTLE INSTRUCTION BOOK

## FOR THE CLASS OF 2010

# GOD'S LITTLE INSTRUCTION BOOK

## FOR THE CLASS OF 2010

David C Cook®

*transforming lives together*

GOD'S LITTLE INSTRUCTION BOOK FOR THE CLASS OF 2010
Published by David C. Cook
4050 Lee Vance View
Colorado Springs, CO 80918 U.S.A.

David C. Cook Distribution Canada
55 Woodslee Avenue, Paris, Ontario, Canada N3L 3E5

David C. Cook U.K., Kingsway Communications
Eastbourne, East Sussex BN23 6NT, England

Bible credits are located at the back of this book.

ISBN 978-1-4347-0062-9

The Team: Ingrid Beck, Amy Kiechlin, Sarah Schultz, and Jack Campbell
Interior Design: Karen Athen
Cover Design: studiogearbox.com
Cover Photo: Steve Gardner/Pixelworks Studio

Printed in Canada

First Edition 2009

1 2 3 4 5 6 7 8 9 10

122109

# INTRODUCTION

**Congratulations! As a member of the Class of 2010, you are part of a new and changing millennium filled with innovative technologies and amazing discoveries.**

**These exciting times have made the earth a much more challenging and complicated place to live. You will be confronted with opportunities to make wise decisions and to be a shining light in an often dark and confusing place. How do you make good choices when everything around you is moving and changing? And how do you cut through the hype and find what is good and true?**

**In *God's Little Instruction Book for the Class of 2010*, we offer you wisdom sufficient to help you navigate the twenty-first century. We have taken quotes from ordinary people and heroes throughout history and combined them with wisdom from the Bible to help you become the person you aspire to be. We hope the truths presented in these pages will help you settle your life on an unshakable foundation and enable you to help build a world filled with infinite possibilities.**

FOR THE CLASS OF **2010**

The best thing about the future is that
it comes only one day at a time.
—ABRAHAM LINCOLN

**Don't be anxious about tomorrow. God
will take care of your tomorrow too.
Live one day at a time.**

**Matthew 6:34** TLB

FOR THE CLASS OF 2010

Anxiety does not empty tomorrow of its sorrows,
but only empties today of its strength.
—CHARLES H. SPURGEON

**Cast your cares on the LORD and he
will sustain you.**

**Psalm 55:22**

We have a God who delights in impossibilities.
—Andrew Murray

**Jesus said to them, "With people this is impossible, but with God all things are possible."**

**Matthew 19:26** NASB

FOR THE CLASS OF 2010

You may laugh out loud in the future at something you're eating your heart out over today.
—CHARLES R. SWINDOLL

**Our light affliction, which is but for a moment, is working for us a far more exceeding and eternal weight of glory.**

**2 Corinthians 4:17** NKJV

FOR THE CLASS OF 2010

God is the God of promise. He keeps His word, even when that seems impossible; even when the circumstances seem to point to the opposite.
—COLIN URQUHART

**What I have said, that will I bring about; what I have planned, that will I do.**

**Isaiah 46:11**

FOR THE CLASS OF 2010

We never test the resources of God
until we attempt the impossible.
—F. B. MEYER

**Now faith is being sure of what we
hope for and certain of what we do not
see.**

**Hebrews 11:1**

FOR THE CLASS OF 2010

To just read the Bible, attend church, and avoid "big" sins—is this passionate, wholehearted love for God?
—FRANÇOIS FÉNELON

**Let's see how inventive we can be in encouraging love and helping out, not avoiding worshiping together as some do but spurring each other on, especially as we see the big Day approaching.**

**Hebrews 10:24–25 MSG**

FOR THE CLASS OF 2010

Laughter adds richness, texture, and color
to otherwise ordinary days. It is a gift,
a choice, a discipline, and an art.
—TIM HANSEL

**A time to weep, and a time to laugh; a
time to mourn, and a time to dance.**

**Ecclesiastes 3:4** NKJV

FOR THE CLASS OF 2010

Truth and oil always come to the surface.
—SPANISH PROVERB

When he, the Spirit of truth, comes, he will guide you into all truth…. He will tell you what is yet to come.

John 16:13

FOR THE CLASS OF 2010

When you feel yourself most indisposed to prayer
do not yield to it, but strive and endeavor to
pray even when you think you cannot pray.
—ARTHUR HILDERSHAM

**Pray continually.**

**1 Thessalonians 5:17**

FOR THE CLASS OF 2010

Always do right. This will gratify some people and astonish the rest.
—MARK TWAIN

**This is a trustworthy saying, and I want you to insist on these teachings so that all who trust in God will devote themselves to doing good. These teachings are good and beneficial for everyone.**

**Titus 3:8 NLT**

FOR THE CLASS OF 2010

We are all faced with a series of great opportunities brilliantly disguised as impossible situations.
—CHARLES R. SWINDOLL

**Fight the good fight of the faith. Take hold of the eternal life to which you were called when you made your good confession in the presence of many witnesses.**

**1 Timothy 6:12**

FOR THE CLASS OF 2010

Colors fade, temples crumble, empires
fall, but wise words endure.
—EDWARD THORNDIKE

**The grass withers, the flower fades, but
the word of our God stands forever.**

**Isaiah 40:8 NKJV**

FOR THE CLASS OF 2010

Everything that is done in the world is done by hope.
—MARTIN LUTHER

**Find rest, O my soul, in God alone; my hope comes from him.**

**Psalm 62:5**

FOR THE CLASS OF 2010

No man ever became wise by chance.
—SENECA

**Hold on to instruction, do not let it go; guard it well, for it is your life.**

**Proverbs 4:13**

FOR THE CLASS OF 2010

If you keep watch over your hearts, and listen for the Voice of God and learn of Him, in one short hour you can learn more from Him than you could learn from Man in a thousand years.

—JOHANNES TAULER

**True wisdom and real power belong to God; from him we learn how to live, and also what to live for.**

**Job 12:13** MSG

FOR THE CLASS OF 2010

Time is the deposit each one has in the bank of God, and no one knows the balance.
—R. W. SOCKMAN

**The day is yours, and yours also the night; you established the sun and moon.**

**Psalm 74:16**

FOR THE CLASS OF 2010

Fire is the test of gold; adversity, of strong men.
—Martha Graham

**Blessed is the man who perseveres under trial, because when he has stood the test, he will receive the crown of life that God has promised to those who love him.**

**James 1:12**

FOR THE CLASS OF 2010

Things are not always what they seem.

—AUTHOR UNKNOWN

**God does not see the same way people see. People look at the outside of a person, but the LORD looks at the heart.**

**1 Samuel 16:7 NCV**

Death is more universal than life. Every man dies; not every man really lives.
—A. SACHS

**I have come that they may have life, and have it to the full.**

**John 10:10**

FOR THE CLASS OF 2010

Wise men are not always silent,
but they know when to be.
—AUTHOR UNKNOWN

**Desire without knowledge is not good,
and to be overhasty is to sin and miss
the mark.**

**Proverbs 19:2 AB**

FOR THE CLASS OF 2010

The only thing we have to fear is fear itself.
—FRANKLIN D. ROOSEVELT

**God is our refuge and strength, an ever-present help in trouble. Therefore we will not fear.**

**Psalm 46:1–2**

FOR THE CLASS OF 2010

The value of life lies not in the length of days, but in the use we make of them.
—MICHEL DE MONTAIGNE

**Be careful how you live. Don't live like fools, but like those who are wise. Make the most of every opportunity.**

**Ephesians 5:15–16 NLT**

FOR THE CLASS OF 2010

When one door closes another door opens.
—ALEXANDER GRAHAM BELL

**Let your eyes look straight ahead, fix your gaze directly before you.**

**Proverbs 4:25**

FOR THE CLASS OF **2010**

The test of courage comes when we are in the minority. The test of tolerance comes when we are in the majority.

—R. W. SOCKMAN

**Watch, stand fast in the faith, be brave, be strong. Let all that you do be done with love.**

1 Corinthians 16:13–14 NKJV

FOR THE CLASS OF 2010

There is nothing we can do to make
God love us more; there is nothing we
can do to make God love us less.
—PHILIP YANCEY

**Long ago the LORD said to Israel: "I
have loved you, my people, with an
everlasting love. With unfailing love I
have drawn you to myself."**

**Jeremiah 31:3 NLT**

FOR THE CLASS OF 2010

Every oak tree started out as a couple
of nuts who stood their ground.

—AUTHOR UNKNOWN

**My dear brothers, stand firm. Let
nothing move you. Always give
yourselves fully to the work of the
Lord, because you know that your
labor in the Lord is not in vain.**

**1 Corinthians 15:58**

FOR THE CLASS OF 2010

There can be no such thing as a necessary evil. For if a thing is really necessary, it cannot be an evil and if it is an evil, it is not necessary.

—TIORIO

**This is what the LORD says: "Stand at the crossroads and look; ask for the ancient paths, ask where the good way is, and walk in it, and you will find rest for your souls."**

**Jeremiah 6:16**

FOR THE CLASS OF 2010

Life is a journey, not a destination. Happiness is not "there" but here, not "tomorrow" but today.
—SIDNEY GREENBERG

**Do not boast about tomorrow, for you do not know what a day may bring forth.**

**Proverbs 27:1** NASB

FOR THE CLASS OF 2010

I try to avoid looking forward or backward,
and try to keep looking upward.
—CHARLOTTE BRONTË

**I have set the LORD always before me.
Because he is at my right hand, I will
not be shaken.**

**Psalm 16:8**

FOR THE CLASS OF 2010

Courage is fear that has said its prayers.
—DOROTHY BERNARD

**I have told you these things, so that in me you may have peace. In this world you will have trouble. But take heart! I have overcome the world.**

**John 16:33**

FOR THE CLASS OF 2010

When we long for life without difficulties,
remind us that oaks grow strong in contrary
winds and diamonds are made under pressure.
—PETER MARSHALL

**You must learn to endure everything,
so that you will be completely mature
and not lacking in anything.**

**James 1:4 CEV**

FOR THE CLASS OF 2010

What the caterpillar calls the end of the
world, the master calls a butterfly.
—RICHARD BACH

**We, who with unveiled faces all reflect
the Lord's glory, are being transformed
into his likeness with ever-increasing
glory.**

**2 Corinthians 3:18**

FOR THE CLASS OF 2010

God will not demand more from you than you can do. Whatever God asks of you, he will give you the strength to do.

—AUTHOR UNKNOWN

**He said to me, "My grace is sufficient for you, for my power is made perfect in weakness." Therefore I will boast all the more gladly about my weaknesses, so that Christ's power may rest on me.**

**2 Corinthians 12:9**

FOR THE CLASS OF 2010

Have courage for the great sorrows of life
and patience for the small ones; and when
you have laboriously accomplished your daily
task, go to sleep in peace. God is awake.
—Victor Hugo

**He will not allow your foot to slip; He
who keeps you will not slumber.**

**Psalm 121:3 NASB**

FOR THE CLASS OF 2010

Five great enemies to peace inhabit with us:
avarice, ambition, envy, anger, and pride.
—FRANCESCO PETRARCH

**The LORD will bless His people with peace.**

**Psalm 29:11** NKJV

FOR THE CLASS OF 2010

When you come to the end of your
rope, tie a knot and hang on.
—FRANKLIN D. ROOSEVELT

**Consider it pure joy, my brothers,
whenever you face trials of many
kinds, because you know that
the testing of your faith develops
perseverance.**

**James 1:2–3**

FOR THE CLASS OF 2010

God's love for us is proclaimed with each sunrise.
—AUTHOR UNKNOWN

He has made everything beautiful in its time. He has also set eternity in the hearts of men; yet they cannot fathom what God has done from beginning to end.

Ecclesiastes 3:11

FOR THE CLASS OF 2010

To accomplish great things, we
must dream as well as act.
—ANATOLE FRANCE

**I praise the Lord because he advises
me. Even at night, I feel his leading.**

**Psalm 16:7 NCV**

FOR THE CLASS OF 2010

It is later than you think.
—ROBERT SERVICE

**The night is far spent, the day is at hand. Therefore let us cast off the works of darkness, and let us put on the armor of light.**

**Romans 13:12** NKJV

FOR THE CLASS OF **2010**

A ship in harbor is safe, but that is
not what ships are built for.
—JOHN A. SHEDD

**You are the world's light—a city on a
hill, glowing in the night for all to see.
Don't hide your light!**

**Matthew 5:14–15 TLB**

FOR THE CLASS OF 2010

Real prayer comes not from gritting
our teeth but from falling in love.
—RICHARD FOSTER

**By day the LORD directs his love, at
night his song is with me—a prayer to
the God of my life.**

**Psalm 42:8**

FOR THE CLASS OF 2010

Wisdom is the combination of honesty and
knowledge applied through experience.
—AUTHOR UNKNOWN

**Teach us to number our days aright,
that we may gain a heart of wisdom.**

**Psalm 90:12**

FOR THE CLASS OF 2010

God does not love us because we are valuable.
We are valuable because God loves us!
—MARTIN LUTHER

**The Lord takes pleasure in those who reverently and worshipfully fear Him, in those who hope in His mercy and loving-kindness.**

**Psalm 147:11** AB

FOR THE CLASS OF 2010

What is a friend? A single soul dwelling in two bodies.
—ARISTOTLE

**Jonathan was deeply impressed with David—an immediate bond was forged between them. He became totally committed to David. From that point on he would be David's number-one advocate and friend.**

**1 Samuel 18:1 MSG**

FOR THE CLASS OF 2010

The world is governed more by
appearance than realities.
—DANIEL WEBSTER

**These are a shadow of the things that
were to come; the reality, however, is
found in Christ.**

**Colossians 2:17**

A good laugh is sunshine in a house.
—WILLIAM MAKEPEACE THACKERAY

**A joyful heart is good medicine.**

**Proverbs 17:22 NASB**

FOR THE CLASS OF 2010

Life can only be understood backwards;
but it must be lived forwards.
—SØREN KIERKEGAARD

**This is what the LORD says—your
Redeemer, the Holy One of Israel: "I
am the LORD your God, who teaches
you what is best for you, who directs
you in the way you should go."**

**Isaiah 48:17**

FOR THE CLASS OF 2010

Good is silent, discreet, unassuming, whereas evil is so noisy. We only hear about the evil in the world.

—Isabel Allende

**Be still in the presence of the Lord, and wait patiently for him to act. Don't worry about evil people who prosper or fret about their wicked schemes.**

**Psalm 37:7 NLT**

FOR THE CLASS OF 2010

Men are not against you; they are
merely for themselves.
—GENE FOWLER

**Bear with each other and forgive
whatever grievances you may have
against one another. Forgive as the
Lord forgave you.**

**Colossians 3:13**

FOR THE CLASS OF 2010

When you were born, you cried and the world rejoiced. Live your life in such a manner that when you die the world cries and you rejoice.

—INDIAN PROVERB

**For to me, living means living for Christ, and dying is even better.**

**Philippians 1:21** NLT

FOR THE CLASS OF **2010**

Things do not happen in this world—
they are brought about.
—AUTHOR UNKNOWN

**Heaven and earth will pass away, but my words will never pass away.**

**Luke 21:33**

I am not afraid of tomorrow, for I have
seen yesterday and I love today.
—WILLIAM ALLEN WHITE

**Whoever trusts in the LORD shall be
safe.**

**Proverbs 29:25** NKJV

FOR THE CLASS OF 2010

Keep trying to win; keep playing the game;
but keep room in your heart for a song.

—AUTHOR UNKNOWN

**He put a new song in my mouth, a hymn of praise to our God.**

**Psalm 40:3**

FOR THE CLASS OF 2010

The greater part of our happiness or misery depends on our disposition and not our circumstances.
—MARTHA WASHINGTON

**I know how to live on almost nothing or with everything. I have learned the secret of contentment in every situation.**

**Philippians 4:12 TLB**

FOR THE CLASS OF **2010**

A candle loses nothing by lighting another candle.
—PROVERB

**Carry each other's burdens, and in this way you will fulfill the law of Christ.**

**Galatians 6:2**

Take time to deliberate; but when the time
for action arrives, stop thinking and go in.
—ANDREW JACKSON

**Rise up; this matter is in your hands.
We will support you, so take courage
and do it.**

**Ezra 10:4**

FOR THE CLASS OF **2010**

Constant prayer will only "burden" us
as wings burden the bird in flight.
—DALLAS WILLARD

**Those who wait upon God get fresh
strength. They spread their wings and
soar like eagles.**

**Isaiah 40:31 MSG**

FOR THE CLASS OF 2010

Who lives in fear is no free man.
—HORACE

**The LORD is with me; I will not be afraid.**

**Psalm 118:6**

FOR THE CLASS OF 2010

When I pray, coincidences happen,
and when I do not, they don't.
—WILLIAM TEMPLE

**All things you ask in prayer, believing, you will receive.**

**Matthew 21:22 NASB**

FOR THE CLASS OF 2010

Think of these things, whence you came, where you are going, and to whom you must account.

—BENJAMIN FRANKLIN

**So then each of us shall give account of himself to God.**

**Romans 14:12** NKJV

FOR THE CLASS OF 2010

We live in deeds, not years; in thoughts, not breaths; in feelings not figures on a dial. We should count time by heart throbs. He most lives who thinks most, feels noblest, acts the best.
—PHILIP JAMES BAILEY

**"In him we live and move and have our being." As some of your own poets have said, "We are his offspring."**

**Acts 17:28**

FOR THE CLASS OF 2010

To speak painful truth through loving
words, that is friendship.
—HENRY WARD BEECHER

**Faithful are the wounds of a friend.**

**Proverbs 27:6** NKJV

FOR THE CLASS OF 2010

No passion so effectually robs the mind of all
its powers of acting and reasoning as fear.
—EDMUND BURKE

**You will keep in perfect peace him
whose mind is steadfast, because he
trusts in you.**

**Isaiah 26:3**

FOR THE CLASS OF 2010

Blessed are those who see the hand of God in the haphazard, inexplicable, and seemingly senseless circumstances of life.

—AUTHOR UNKNOWN

**I am with you, and I will protect you wherever you go.**

**Genesis 28:15** NLT

FOR THE CLASS OF 2010

It's a good thing to have all the props pulled out from under us occasionally. It gives us some sense of what is rock under our feet, and what is sand.

—MADELEINE L'ENGLE

**He is the Rock, his works are perfect, and all his ways are just. A faithful God who does no wrong, upright and just is he.**

**Deuteronomy 32:4**

FOR THE CLASS OF 2010

A great deal of talent is lost to the
world for want of a little courage.
—SYDNEY SMITH

**The LORD is on my side; I will not fear.
What can man do to me?**

**Psalm 118:6 NKJV**

FOR THE CLASS OF 2010

One today is worth two tomorrows.
—BENJAMIN FRANKLIN

**Since no man knows the future, who can tell him what is to come?**

**Ecclesiastes 8:7**

FOR THE CLASS OF 2010

God dwells in eternity but time dwells in
God. He has already lived all our tomorrows
as He has lived all our yesterdays.
—A. W. Tozer

**I will be with you always, even until
the end of the world.**

**Matthew 28:20 CEV**

FOR THE CLASS OF 2010

The world is charged with the grandeur of God.
—GERARD MANLEY HOPKINS

**You alone are the LORD. You made the heavens ... and all their starry host, the earth and all that is on it.... You give life to everything.**

**Nehemiah 9:6**

FOR THE CLASS OF 2010

I have learned over the years that when one's mind is made up, this diminishes fear; knowing what must be done does away with fear.
—Rosa Parks

**You shall know the truth, and the truth shall make you free.**

**John 8:32** NKJV

FOR THE CLASS OF 2010

Do all the good you can,
By all the means you can,
In all the ways you can,
In all the places you can,
At all the times you can,
To all the people you can,
As long as ever you can.
—JOHN WESLEY

**Do not forget to do good and to share with others, for with such sacrifices God is pleased.**

**Hebrews 13:16**

FOR THE CLASS OF 2010

Hope means simply the belief that something good lies ahead. It is not the same as optimism or wishful thinking, for these imply a denial of reality.
—PHILIP YANCEY

**There is surely a future hope for you, and your hope will not be cut off.**

**Proverbs 23:18**

FOR THE CLASS OF 2010

One must always have one's boots
on and be ready to go.
—MICHEL DE MONTAIGNE

**You also must be ready all the time, for
the Son of Man will come when least
expected.**

**Luke 12:40** NLT

FOR THE CLASS OF 2010

If you can't change your circumstances,
change the way you respond to them.
—AUTHOR UNKNOWN

**We know that in all things God works
for the good of those who love him,
who have been called according to his
purpose.**

**Romans 8:28**

FOR THE CLASS OF 2010

It often happens that those of whom we speak
least on earth are best known in heaven.

—NICOLAS CAUSSIN

**You are the ones chosen by God, chosen for the high calling of priestly work, chosen to be a holy people, God's instruments to do his work and speak out for him.**

**1 Peter 2:9 MSG**

FOR THE CLASS OF 2010

Don't forget in the darkness what
you have learned in the light.
—Joseph T. Bayly

**Remember those earlier days after you
had received the light, when you stood
your ground in a great contest in the
face of suffering.**

**Hebrews 10:32**

FOR THE CLASS OF 2010

Never spend your money before you have it.
—THOMAS JEFFERSON

**Render to all what is due them.... Owe nothing to anyone except to love one another.**

**Romans 13:7–8** NASB

FOR THE CLASS OF **2010**

If God maintains sun and planets in bright
and ordered beauty, he can keep us.
—F. B. MEYER

**If I rise on the wings of the dawn, if I
settle on the far side of the sea, even
there your hand will guide me, your
right hand will hold me fast.**

**Psalm 139:9–10**

FOR THE CLASS OF 2010

I am an old man and have known a great many troubles, but most of them never happened.
—MARK TWAIN

**In peace I will lie down and sleep, for you alone, O LORD, will keep me safe.**

**Psalm 4:8 NLT**

FOR THE CLASS OF 2010

Happiness depends on what happens; joy does not.
—OSWALD CHAMBERS

**You have made known to me the path of life; you will fill me with joy in your presence, with eternal pleasures at your right hand.**

**Psalm 16:11**

FOR THE CLASS OF 2010

God takes life's pieces and gives us unbroken peace.
—W. D. GOUGH

**The peace of God, which surpasses all understanding, will guard your hearts and minds through Christ Jesus.**

**Philippians 4:7** NKJV

Without God the world would be
a maze without a clue.
—WOODROW WILSON

**For that is what God is like. He is
our God forever and ever, and he will
guide us until we die.**

**Psalm 48:14 NLT**

FOR THE CLASS OF 2010

The most revolutionary statement in
history is "Love thy enemy."
—ELDRIDGE CLEAVER

**Love your enemies! Pray for those who
persecute you! In that way, you will be
acting as true children of your Father
in heaven. For he gives his sunlight
to both the evil and the good, and he
sends rain on the just and the unjust
alike.**

**Matthew 5:44–45** NLT

FOR THE CLASS OF 2010

Peace is not an absence of war, it is a virtue, a state of mind, a disposition for benevolence, confidence, justice.
—BARUCH SPINOZA

**Seek peace and pursue it.**

**Psalm 34:14**

FOR THE CLASS OF 2010

Three things for which thanks are due:
an invitation, a gift, and a warning.
—WELSH PROVERB

**Oh, give thanks to the LORD, for He is
good! For His mercy endures forever.**

**1 Chronicles 16:34 NKJV**

FOR THE CLASS OF 2010

Within your heart
Keep one still, secret spot
Where dreams may go.
—LOUISE DRISCOLL

**Above all else, guard your heart, for it is the wellspring of life.**

**Proverbs 4:23**

FOR THE CLASS OF 2010

God's investment in us is so great he could not possibly abandon us.
—ERWIN LUTZER

**The LORD appeared to him from afar, saying, "I have loved you with an everlasting love; therefore I have drawn you with lovingkindness."**

**Jeremiah 31:3 NASB**

FOR THE CLASS OF 2010

Why does God always use dreams, intuition, memory, phone calls, vague stirrings in my heart? I would say that this *really* doesn't work for me at all. Except that it does.
—ANNE LAMOTT

**Whether you turn to the right or to the left, your ears will hear a voice behind you, saying, "This is the way; walk in it."**

**Isaiah 30:21**

FOR THE CLASS OF 2010

Sometimes I think I understand everything,
then I regain consciousness.
—Ray Bradbury

**Trust in the Lord with all your
heart, and lean not on your own
understanding; in all your ways
acknowledge Him, and He shall direct
your paths.**

**Proverbs 3:5–6 NKJV**

Debt is the worst poverty.
—M. G. LICHTWER

**The borrower is servant to the lender.**

**Proverbs 22:7**

FOR THE CLASS OF 2010

People say, "What is the sense of our small effort?" They cannot see that we must lay one brick at a time, take one step at a time.
—DOROTHY DAY

**Go to the ant.... Consider her ways and be wise.**

**Proverbs 6:6** NKJV

Fear defeats more people than any
other one thing in the world.
—RALPH WALDO EMERSON


**Perfect love drives out fear.**

1 John 4:18


FOR THE CLASS OF **2010**

There are always uncertainties ahead, but there is always one certainty—God's will is good.
—VERNON PATERSON

**Let God transform you into a new person by changing the way you think. Then you will learn to know God's will for you, which is good and pleasing and perfect.**

**Romans 12:2 NLT**

FOR THE CLASS OF 2010

Never fear shadows. They simply mean
there's a light shining somewhere nearby.
—RUTH E. RENKEL

**Though I walk through the valley of
the shadow of death, I will fear no evil;
for You are with me.**

**Psalm 23:4** NKJV

FOR THE CLASS OF **2010**

On days when life is difficult and I feel overwhelmed, as I do fairly often, it helps to remember in my prayers that all God requires of me is to trust Him and be His friend. I find I can do that.

—BRUCE LARSON

No, O people, the LORD has told you what is good, and this is what he requires of you: to do what is right, to love mercy, and to walk humbly with your God.

Micah 6:8 NLT

FOR THE CLASS OF 2010

The cure for fear is faith.
—Lena Kellogg Sadler

**I sought the Lord, and he answered
me; he delivered me from all my fears.**

**Psalm 34:4**

FOR THE CLASS OF 2010

We can do no great things, only
small things with great love.
—MOTHER TERESA

[Jesus said,] "Give a cool cup of water
to someone who is thirsty, for instance.
The smallest act of giving or receiving
makes you a true apprentice. You
won't lose out on a thing."

**Matthew 10:42 MSG**

FOR THE CLASS OF 2010

Let your hopes, not your hurts, shape your future.
—ROBERT H. SCHULLER

**Why am I discouraged? Why is my heart so sad? I will put my hope in God! I will praise him again—my Savior and my God!**

**Psalm 43:5** NLT

FOR THE CLASS OF 2010

All I have seen teaches me to trust the
Creator for all I have not seen.
—Ralph Waldo Emerson

**I will say of the Lord, "He is my refuge
and my fortress, my God, in whom I
trust."**

**Psalm 91:2**

FOR THE CLASS OF 2010

I would rather walk with God in the
dark than go alone in the light.
—MARY GARDINER BRAINARD

**Though He slay me, yet will I trust
Him.**

**Job 13:15** NKJV

FOR THE CLASS OF 2010

God never put anyone in a place too small to grow in.
—Henrietta Mears

**Give thanks in all circumstances, for this is God's will for you in Christ Jesus.**

**1 Thessalonians 5:18**

FOR THE CLASS OF 2010

Act boldly and unseen forces will come to your aid.
—DOROTHEA BRANDE

**We have the Lord our God to fight our battles for us!**

**2 Chronicles 32:8** TLB

FOR THE CLASS OF 2010

Courage is the power to let go of the familiar.
—RAYMOND LINDQUIST

**The LORD is the stronghold of my life—
of whom shall I be afraid?**

**Psalm 27:1**

FOR THE CLASS OF 2010

Do not let what you cannot do
interfere with what you can do.
—John Wooden

**Everything is possible for him who
believes.**

**Mark 9:23**

FOR THE CLASS OF 2010

Fear grows in darkness; if you think there's a bogeyman around, turn on the light.

—Dorothy Thompson

You, Lord, are the light that keeps me safe. I am not afraid of anyone. You protect me, and I have no fears.

Psalm 27:1 CEV

FOR THE CLASS OF 2010

You just need to be a flea against injustice. Enough committed fleas biting strategically can make even the biggest dog uncomfortable and transform even the biggest nation.

—MARIAN WRIGHT EDELMAN

**You hear, O LORD, the desire of the afflicted; you encourage them, and you listen to their cry, defending the fatherless and the oppressed, in order that man, who is of the earth, may terrify no more.**

**Psalm 10:17–18**

FOR THE CLASS OF 2010

Keep your fears to yourself, but share
your courage with others.
—ROBERT LOUIS STEVENSON

**Honor Christ and let him be the Lord
of your life. Always be ready to give an
answer when someone asks you about
your hope.**

**1 Peter 3:15 CEV**

Trust the past to the mercy of God, the present to His love, and the future to His providence.

—Saint Augustine

**Be strong and courageous. Do not be terrified; do not be discouraged, for the Lord your God will be with you wherever you go.**

**Joshua 1:9**

FOR THE CLASS OF 2010

Truth, like surgery, may hurt, but it cures.
—HAN SUYIN

**Speaking the truth in love, we will in all things grow up into him who is the Head, that is, Christ.**

**Ephesians 4:15**

The capacity to care is the thing which
gives life its deepest significance.
—PABLO CASALS

**Bear one another's burdens, and
thereby fulfill the law of Christ.**

**Galatians 6:2 NASB**

FOR THE CLASS OF 2010

No person has the right to rain on your dreams.
—MARIAN WRIGHT EDELMAN

**I can do all things through Christ who strengthens me.**

**Philippians 4:13** NKJV

FOR THE CLASS OF **2010**

God loves each of us as if there were only one of us.
—Saint Augustine

**Christ's love compels us, because we are convinced that one died for all.**

**2 Corinthians 5:14**

FOR THE CLASS OF 2010

It is amidst great perils that we see brave hearts.
—JEAN-FRANÇOIS REGNARD

**Then I'm up again—rested, tall and steady, fearless before the enemy mobs coming at me from all sides.**

**Psalm 3:6 MSG**

FOR THE CLASS OF 2010

The mind grows by what it feeds on.
—J. G. HOLLAND

**The mind controlled by the Spirit is life and peace.**

**Romans 8:6**

FOR THE CLASS OF 2010

Trust in yourself and you are doomed to disappointment; … but trust in God, and you are never to be confounded in time or eternity.
—D. L. Moody

**It is better to trust in the Lord than to put confidence in man.**

**Psalm 118:8 NKJV**

FOR THE CLASS OF 2010

To believe in God is to know that all the rules will be fair, and that there will be wonderful surprises!
—UGO BETTI

**The Rock: His works are perfect, and the way he works is fair and just.**

**Deuteronomy 32:4 MSG**

FOR THE CLASS OF 2010

Don't count on your education to make you wise.
—AUTHOR UNKNOWN

**He who trusts in himself is a fool, but
he who walks in wisdom is kept safe.**

**Proverbs 28:26**

FOR THE CLASS OF 2010

Don't fear change—embrace it.
—ANTHONY J. D'ANGELO

I am leaving you with a gift—peace of
mind and heart! And the peace I give
isn't fragile like the peace the world
gives. So don't be troubled or afraid.

John 14:27 TLB

FOR THE CLASS OF 2010

Most of the verses written about praise in God's Word were voiced by people faced with crushing heartaches, injustice, treachery, slander, and scores of other difficult situations.

—JONI EARECKSON TADA

**David sang to the LORD ... when the LORD delivered him from the hand of all his enemies.... He said: "The LORD is my rock, my fortress and my deliverer."**

**2 Samuel 22:1–2**

FOR THE CLASS OF 2010

First keep the peace within yourself, then
you can also bring peace to others.
—THOMAS À KEMPIS

**Blessed are the peacemakers, for they
will be called sons of God.**

**Matthew 5:9**

FOR THE CLASS OF 2010

You can't test courage cautiously.
—Annie Dillard

**Whatever you do, do it heartily, as to the Lord and not to men.**

**Colossians 3:23** NKJV

FOR THE CLASS OF **2010**

Do not seek to follow in the footsteps of the men of old; seek what they sought.
—MATSUO BASHŌ

**I love everyone who loves me, and I will be found by all who honestly search.**

**Proverbs 8:17** CEV

FOR THE CLASS OF 2010

Success consists of getting up just
one more time than you fall.
—OLIVER GOLDSMITH

**I can do everything through him who
gives me strength.**

**Philippians 4:13**

FOR THE CLASS OF 2010

Snuggle in God's arms. When you are hurting, when you feel lonely, left out. Let Him cradle you, comfort you, reassure you of His all-sufficient power and love.

—KAY ARTHUR

**Let, I pray, Your merciful kindness be for my comfort.**

**Psalm 119:76** NKJV

FOR THE CLASS OF 2010

The stars are constantly shining, but often we do not see them until the dark hours.

—AUTHOR UNKNOWN

**My help comes from the LORD, the Maker of heaven and earth.**

**Psalm 121:2**

FOR THE CLASS OF 2010

The heights by great men reached and kept
Were not attained by sudden flight,
But they, while their companions slept,
Were toiling upward in the night.
—HENRY WADSWORTH LONGFELLOW

**So let's not get tired of doing what is good. At just the right time we will reap a harvest of blessing if we don't give up.**

**Galatians 6:9** NLT

FOR THE CLASS OF 2010

I have decided to stick with love. Hate
is too great a burden to bear.
—MARTIN LUTHER KING JR.

**Do everything in love.**

**1 Corinthians 16:14**

FOR THE CLASS OF 2010

Anything I've ever done that ultimately was
worthwhile initially scared me to death.
—BETTY BENDER

**I would have despaired unless I had
believed that I would see the goodness
of the LORD in the land of the living.**

**Psalm 27:13 NASB**

FOR THE CLASS OF 2010

To believe in something, and not
to live it, is dishonest.

—MAHATMA GANDHI

**If we live by the Spirit, let us also walk
by the Spirit.**

**Galatians 5:25** NASB

FOR THE CLASS OF **2010**

To trust in Him when no need is pressing, when things seem going right of themselves, may be harder than when things seem going wrong.
—GEORGE MACDONALD

Give me neither poverty nor riches, but give me only my daily bread. Otherwise, I may have too much and disown you and say, "Who is the LORD?" Or I may become poor and steal, and so dishonor the name of my God.

Proverbs 30:8–9

FOR THE CLASS OF 2010

Some debts are fun when you are acquiring them, but none are fun when you set about retiring them.
—OGDEN NASH

**Why do you spend money for what is not bread, and your wages for what does not satisfy? Listen carefully to Me, and eat what is good, and delight yourself in abundance.**

**Isaiah 55:2 NASB**

FOR THE CLASS OF 2010

Do exactly what you would do if you felt most secure.
—MEISTER ECKEHART

**Have not I commanded you? Be strong, vigorous, and very courageous. Be not afraid, neither be dismayed, for the Lord your God is with you wherever you go.**

**Joshua 1:9** AB

FOR THE CLASS OF 2010

The little troubles and worries of life may be as stumbling blocks in our way, or we may make them stepping-stones to a nobler character and to Heaven. Troubles are often the tools by which God fashions us for better things.

—HENRY WARD BEECHER

**No discipline is enjoyable while it is happening—it's painful! But afterward there will be a peaceful harvest of right living for those who are trained in this way.**

**Hebrews 12:11 NLT**

FOR THE CLASS OF 2010

In His will is our peace.
—DANTE ALIGHIERI

**Great peace have those who love Your law, and nothing causes them to stumble.**

**Psalm 119:165** NKJV

FOR THE CLASS OF **2010**

Never be afraid to trust an unknown
future to a known God.
—Corrie ten Boom

**I will turn the darkness into light
before them and make the rough places
smooth.**

**Isaiah 42:16**

FOR THE CLASS OF 2010

The future is as bright as the promises of God.
—WILLIAM CAREY

**Whatever God has promised gets stamped with the Yes of Jesus.**

**2 Corinthians 1:20 MSG**

FOR THE CLASS OF 2010

Where fear is present, wisdom cannot be.
—Lucius C. Lactantius

**The Lord is my light and my salvation—whom shall I fear?**

**Psalm 27:1**

FOR THE CLASS OF 2010

I am convinced that faith sometimes means
knowing God can, whether or not He does.
—BETH MOORE

**The God we worship can save us from
you and your flaming furnace. But even
if he doesn't, we still won't worship
your gods and the gold statue you have
set up.**

**Daniel 3:17–18** CEV

FOR THE CLASS OF 2010

Do not borrow trouble by dreading
tomorrow. It is the dark menace of the
future that makes cowards of us all.
—DOROTHY DIX

**For he will order his angels to protect
you wherever you go.**

**Psalm 91:11** NLT

FOR THE CLASS OF 2010

To love what you do and feel that it matters—
how could anything be more fun?
—KATHARINE GRAHAM

**For my heart rejoiced in all my labor.**

**Ecclesiastes 2:10 NKJV**

FOR THE CLASS OF 2010

My faith isn't in the idea that I'm more moral than anybody else. My faith is in the idea that God and His love are greater than whatever sins any of us commit.

—RICH MULLINS

**I sought the LORD, and he answered me; he delivered me from all my fears.**

**Psalm 34:4**

FOR THE CLASS OF 2010

Let your words be the genuine picture of your heart.
—JOHN WESLEY

**My mouth shall speak wisdom, and the meditation of my heart shall give understanding.**

**Psalm 49:3** NKJV

FOR THE CLASS OF 2010

Blessed is the man who finds out which way God is moving and then gets going in the same direction.
—AUTHOR UNKNOWN

**Whether you turn to the right or to the left, your ears will hear a voice behind you, saying, "This is the way; walk in it."**

**Isaiah 30:21**

FOR THE CLASS OF 2010

At the height of laughter, the universe is flung into a kaleidoscope of new possibilities.
—Jean Houston

**He will yet fill your mouth with laughter and your lips with shouts of joy.**

**Job 8:21**

FOR THE CLASS OF 2010

Call on God, but row away from the rocks.
—HUNTER S. THOMPSON

**Wisdom and good judgment
live together, for wisdom knows
where to discover knowledge and
understanding.**

**Proverbs 8:12 TLB**

FOR THE CLASS OF 2010

Smart is believing half of what you hear;
brilliant is knowing which half to believe.
—AUTHOR UNKNOWN

**For wisdom will enter your heart, and
knowledge will fill you with joy.**

**Proverbs 2:10 NLT**

FOR THE CLASS OF 2010

Obedience to the call of Christ nearly always costs everything to two people: the one who is called, and the one who loves that one.

—OSWALD CHAMBERS

**If you will indeed obey My voice and keep My covenant, then you shall be a special treasure to Me above all people; for all the earth is Mine.**

**Exodus 19:5 NKJV**

FOR THE CLASS OF 2010

We need to pay more attention to how we
treat people than to how they treat us.
—Joyce Meyer

**Love others as well as you love
yourself.**

**Mark 12:31** MSG

FOR THE CLASS OF 2010

The most important single ingredient in the formula of success is knowing how to get along with people.
—THEODORE ROOSEVELT

**See that no one pays back evil for evil, but always try to do good to each other and to everyone else.**

**1 Thessalonians 5:15 TLB**

FOR THE CLASS OF 2010

You can give without loving, but you
cannot love without giving.
—AMY CARMICHAEL

**It is more blessed to give than to
receive.**

**Acts 20:35**

FOR THE CLASS OF **2010**

Sainthood lies in the habit of referring
the smallest actions to God.
—C. S. Lewis

**Praise Him for His mighty acts;
praise Him according to His excellent
greatness!**

**Psalm 150:2 NKJV**

FOR THE CLASS OF 2010

Carve your name on hearts, not on marble.
—CHARLES H. SPURGEON

**The only letter I need is you yourselves! ... They can see that you are a letter from Christ, written by us.... Not one carved on stone, but in human hearts.**

**2 Corinthians 3:2–3 TLB**

FOR THE CLASS OF 2010